Wild Weather

Thunderstorm

REVISED AND UPDATED

Heinemann
LIBRARY

Catherine Chambers

www.heinemann.co.uk/library
Visit our website to find out more information about **Heinemann Library** books.

To order:
☎ Phone ++44 (0)1865 888112
🖹 Send a fax to ++44 (0)1865 314091
💻 Visit the Heinemann Bookshop at www.heinemann.co.uk/library to browse our catalogue and order online.

First published in Great Britain by Heinemann Library, Halley Court, Jordan Hill, Oxford OX2 8EJ, part of Harcourt Education. Heinemann is a registered trademark of Harcourt Education.

Editorial: Clare Lewis
Designed: Steve Mead and Q2A
Illustrations: Paul Bale
Picture Research: Tracy Cummins
Production: Julie Carter

Originated by Modern Age Repro
Printed and bound in China by South China Printing Company Limited

10 digit ISBN 0 431 15087 7
13 digit ISBN 978 0 431 15087 1

11 10 09 08 07
10 9 8 7 6 5 4 3 2 1

British Library Cataloguing in Publication Data

Chambers, Catherine
Wild Weather: Thunderstorms. – 2nd Edition – Juvenile literature
551.5′54
A full catalogue record for this book is available from the British Library.

Acknowledgements
The Publishers would like to thank the following for permission to reproduce photographs: Aflo/naturepl.com p12, Associated Press p19, Corbis pp5, 9, 27, 28, Image Bank p24, Eric Nguyen/Jim Reed Photography/Corbis p18, Oxford Scientific Films p25, PA Photos p26, Photodisc p7, 15, 22, Science Photo Library pp4, 11, 16, 29, Stock Market p20, Stone pp6, 10, 14, 17, 21, 23.

Cover photograph of lightning over Arizona, USA reproduced with permission of Ralph Wetmore/Getty Images.

The Publishers would like to thank Mark Rogers and the Met Office for their assistance with the preparation of this book.

Every effort has been made to contact copyright holders of any material reproduced in this book. Any omissions will be rectified in subsequent printings if notice is given to the Publisher.

The paper used to print this book comes from sustainable resources.

Any words appearing in the text in bold, **like this**, are explained in the Glossary.

Contents

What is a thunderstorm?

A thunderstorm is usually a storm of strong winds and heavy rain. Great flashes of lightning light up the sky. Thunder rumbles around.

■ *Lightning flashes can look colourful.*

■ *Thunderstorms can cause a lot of damage.*

The rain from thunderstorms can cause floods.
Hail can smash windows and ruin **crops**.
Lightning can strike trees and houses. Strong
winds can blow down trees and telegraph poles.

Where do thunderstorms happen?

Thunderstorms happen in many parts of the world. A lot of thunderstorms happen where the Sun is very hot and the air is very moist. Many of these areas lie in or near the **Tropics**.

■ *You can see the rain falling from this thundercloud.*

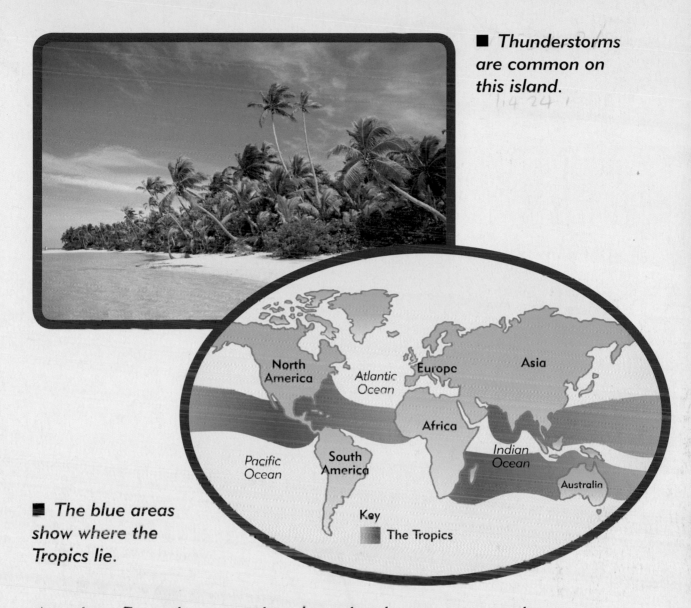

■ *Thunderstorms are common on this island.*

■ *The blue areas show where the Tropics lie.*

North America

Atlantic Ocean

Europe

Asia

Africa

Indian Ocean

Pacific Ocean

South America

Australia

Key

The Tropics

As the Sun heats the land, showers and thunderstorms develop. Thunderstorms can bring heavy rain and strong winds. They can cause a lot of damage.

How do thunderclouds form?

Thunderclouds usually form when there is a lot of **water vapour** in the air. The air feels **humid**. The water vapour rises and cools. Huge clouds form.

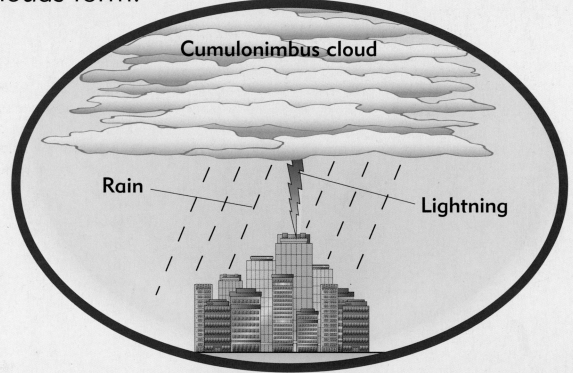

Cumulonimbus cloud

Rain

Lightning

■ *When a cumulonimbus cloud forms there is a thunderstorm.*

■ *Cumulonimbus clouds are tall and dark.*

The clouds that cause thunderstorms are called cumulonimbus. Sometimes they can be as much as 18 kilometres (11 miles) high.

Why do thunderstorms happen?

The droplets of water inside thunderclouds join together. This makes them heavier. They fall to the ground as drops of rain.

■ *Rain often falls over mountains.*

■ *The electricity in a thunderstorm makes lightning.*

Electricity builds up inside the cloud. This electricity is released in a bright flash of lightning. The lightning causes thunder to rumble through the air.

What are lightning and thunder?

Lightning is the bright flash you see when electricity is released from a cloud. There are different types of lightning. The picture shows forked lightning travelling from clouds to the ground.

■ *Lightning travels from the clouds to the ground.*

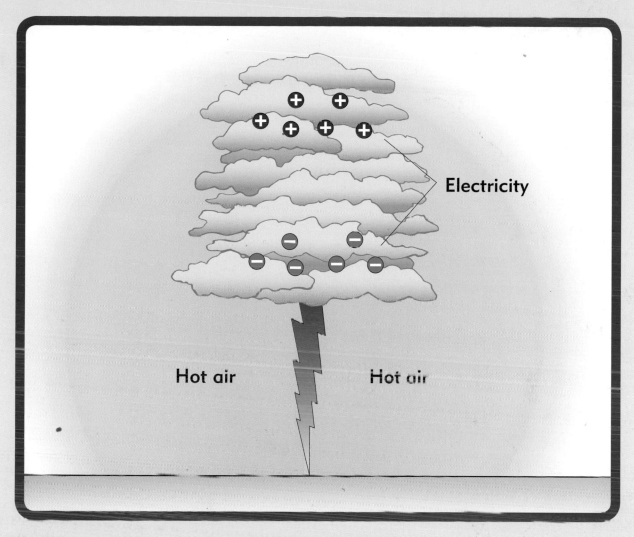

Electricity

Hot air   Hot air

■ *Electricity in the thundercloud makes lightning.*

Thunder is the loud crash you hear when
lightning is released. Lightning heats up
the air very quickly. The air **expands** with
a loud crack.

What are thunderstorms like?

The sky goes very dark before a thunderstorm. Then the wind becomes stronger. Heavy rain starts to pour down.

■ *Heavy rain can make it difficult for drivers to see.*

■ *Lightning flashes across the sky.*

Lightning is followed by thunder. We always hear the thunder after we see the lightning. This is because light travels to us more quickly than sound.

Harmful rain and hail

Lots of rain can fall during a thunderstorm. This can cause **flash floods** in rivers. The water can break bridges. It can trap people in their homes and cars.

■ *This road has flooded.*

■ *Hailstones can do a lot of damage.*

Thunderstorms can also bring balls of ice called
hailstones. Some hailstones are as big as
tennis balls. They can hurt people and animals.
Hailstones can also damage **crops**.

Harmful wind and lightning

Some thunderstorms bring tornadoes. These are tight columns of spinning air. They can damage cars and buildings.

■ *The wind in a tornado is very strong.*

■ *Lightning can cause fires.*

If lightning strikes trees and buildings it can set
fire to them. It can cause forest fires. If lightning
strikes people and animals it can **injure** or
kill them.

Preparing for thunderstorms

People turn off their television sets before a thunderstorm. The lightning can hit the **television aerial** on the roof. It can then move down the aerial and strike the set. This can start a fire, but it doesn't happen very often.

■ *It is best not to watch television during a thunderstorm.*

■ *These cows will be safer on higher ground.*

Thunderstorms can bring strong winds. They can also bring lots of heavy rain. Some farmers move their animals to high ground to save them from floods.

Coping with thunderstorms

Don't stay outside during a thunderstorm! The rain will get you very wet. Lightning can strike buildings and trees. It does not often strike people, but it can.

■ *Tall buildings can be struck by lightning.*

■ *Tall trees can be struck by lightning.*

Trees standing on their own are often struck by lightning. Don't try to **shelter** under trees during a thunderstorm.

Nature and thunderstorms

Animals are often frightened by thunder. They can also get struck by lightning in open fields. Some farmers move their animals under cover during a thunderstorm.

■ *These cows will be safe in their shed.*

■ *Trees can survive being struck by lightning.*

Lightning can strike tree trunks and burn them. Many trees have a sticky gum underneath the **bark**. This oozes out and seals up the burned trunk.

To the rescue!

Heavy rain from thunderstorms can make river waters rise quickly. The water can flood houses and roads. People may need to be rescued by helicopter.

■ *Sometimes helicopters rescue people from the water.*

■ *Firefighters work to put out fires caused by lightning.*

Lightning can set fire to dry trees and plants. This can lead to big forest fires. Firefighters try to put the fire out. They rescue people from the flames.

Adapting to thunderstorms

Metal **lightning conductors** protect buildings from lightning. A metal rod runs down the side of the building. It takes the electricity away from the building and into the ground.

■ *The lightning will strike this rod rather than the building.*

Atlantic Ocean

Europe

Paris
France

Africa

■ *The Eiffel Tower is often struck by lightning.*

This is the Eiffel Tower in Paris, France. Tall buildings like this are more likely to be struck by lightning. Lightning conductors stop people from being hurt by the lightning.

Fact file

◆ A flash of lightning is usually made up of many lightning strokes. They happen so fast that they look like a single flash.

◆ Lightning heats the air around it. It can make it hotter than the surface of the Sun. As the air heats up it makes the sound we call thunder.

◆ There are different types of lightning. Sheet lightning flashes from behind a cloud. Forked lightning has streaks towards the ground.

Glossary

bark hard covering of a tree or bush's trunk and main stems

crops plants grown for food

expand get bigger

flash floods when rain is so heavy that it fills up rivers too quickly and suddenly swamps the land

hail balls of ice that fall from thunderclouds

hailstones (see above)

humid when air contains a lot of moisture

injure hurt

lightning conductor metal rod that picks up the electricity from a lightning strike and takes it down to the ground

shelter keep safe

television aerial set of metal wires that take in television signals. These signals travel to the television set and are changed into pictures and sounds.

Tropics very warm parts of the world on either side of the Equator. The Equator is an imaginary line around the fattest part of the Earth.

water vapour water that has changed into a gas

More books to read

Nature's Patterns: *The Water Cycle*, Monica Hughes (Heinemann
    Library, 2005)
The Weather: *Clouds*, Angela Royston (Chrysalis Children's
    Books, 2004)

Index

Titles in the *Wild Weather* series include:

Hardback 978-0-431-15081-9

Hardback 978-0-431-15082-6

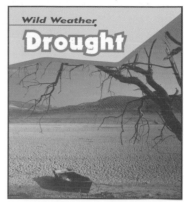

Hardback 978-0-431-15083-3

Hardback 978-0-431-15080-2

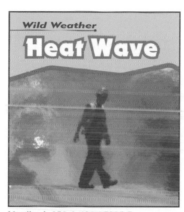

Hardback 978-0-431-15085-7

Hardback 978-0-431-15086-4

Hardback 978-0-431-15087-1

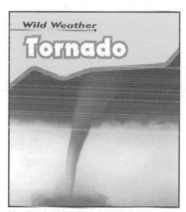

Hardback 978-0-431-15088-8

Find out about other titles Heinemann Library on our website www.heinemann.co.uk/library